FOREWORD

I don't count myself a boat person—I get seasick and, besides, I never quite trust any thin skin to separate me from the deep. Even so, considerable stretches of my life have occurred on what pass as boats of one kind or another. How else does one get around in a country with minimal roads, and where most of the best places lie somewhere in the beyond? (There are airplanes, of course, but the most useful of these float on pontoons.)

For a person without true boat love, an unexpected bounty of boats has accumulated in my Alaskan life. The first, a river kayak I brought to the state a lifetime ago, still sees service at my saltwater fishcamp. For a few years, a flatbottom skiff, with two black dogs standing on its bow, provided basic (i.e., poky) transportation on Kachemak Bay. Then the series of setnet fishing skiffs, from wood to molded fiberglass to aluminum. Then the salmon seiner I spent one (seasick) summer on. And seine skiffs, seine jitney, salmon tenders, various utilitarian rowboats, another kayak. Ferries in winter, a tourboat for looking at tourists, a sailboat in a race, a bunk in a harbor of a strange town.

Did I mention the floatplane? What if I paddle it from a lake shore, anchor it in deep water with a boat anchor, and swim from the pontoons? That lake is my favorite location on earth, and the only other way to put myself among the loons and the lilies, away from tangled shore, is aboard a particular peapod of a wooden rowboat.

Like so much else in America, the boats that serve us get bigger, more specialized, and increasingly industrial; witness, for example, factory trawlers and cruise ships. Alaska's waters float the megaships, as long as football fields, but this delightful book reminds us that our individual lives can still be secured in small, personal, and beloved boats. Boats are dreams—or the vessels of dreams—for drawing a living from the sea, for adventuring, for simply simplifying. Pull in those fish, one by one. Paddle hard. Float.

—Nancy Lord, author of
Green Alaska: Dreams from the Far Coast

CONTENTS

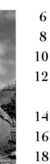

8 A backyard boat production in Ninilchik

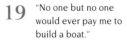

19 "No one but no one would ever pay me to build a boat."

28 Every year Vikings invade Petersburg

38 The fishermen of Kodiak never look a gift blessing in the mouth.

55 The use of at least one roll of duct tape is required on any "boat" entered in the Red Green Regatta.

44 As many as 8,000 visitors a day come to Skagway for a little gold rush ambiance.

62 You can find people aboard the ferry sleeping at almost anytime and almost anywhere.

INTRODUCTION

Besides being the biggest state and the most northern state, Alaska is also a maritime state. Alaska has over 33,900 miles of shoreline that front the Pacific Ocean, the Bering Sea, the Chukchi Sea, and the Beaufort Sea; that's more coastline than all the rest of the Lower 48 states combined. ⚓ Minnesota may boast that it's the "Land of 10,000 Lakes," but Alaska has more than 3,000,000 of them. There are more than 3,000 navigable and not-so-navigable rivers in Alaska, including three of the country's

ten longest rivers: the Yukon at 2,000 miles, the Koyukuk at 554 miles, and the Kuskokwim at 540 miles. And just for good measure, throw in all of the streams, creeks, and ponds scattered over an area one-fifth the size of the rest of the United States. ⚓ Like I said, Alaska is a maritime state. ⚓ The relationship between Alaska and boats goes way back. Mounting evidence indicates that some of the earliest visitors to the New World during the last Ice Age may have arrived by means other than the Bering Land Bridge: it is likely that groups from the Pacific Islands, and perhaps from the mainland of Asia, arrived in North America by boat. Whether anyone arrived specifically by boat in Alaska during that period may never be known, yet it's a distinct possibility. ⚓ Over hundreds, perhaps thousands of years, boats in Alaska have transported people, trading goods, food, tools, traditions, and ideas from place to place. Boats have provided the means by which residents—new and old, Native and non-Native— have harvested the bounties of the northern seas for subsistence. As the Alaskan economy has shifted from subsistence to cash, boats have offered Alaskans economic opportunities through fishing, logging, mineral and oil extraction, and tourism. Through it all, boats have given Alaskans untold hours of simple pleasure. ⚓ Inevitably, along with commerce and pleasure comes fear and risk. Alaska's waters can exact a terrible price: the sea is a wondrous and dreadful place, and the cold swift rivers are filled with their own unique dangers. Through the centuries, untold numbers of Alaska Natives have gone to sea to hunt whale, walrus, and seals, and have never returned. According to the U.S. Department of Labor, commercial fishing is now the most dangerous job in America, exceeding even the dangers of deep-shaft coal mining. ⚓ Many rafters, canoeists,

and kayakers have challenged Alaska's rivers and have drowned. In the nineteenth century, steamships, clipper ships, and freighters plied Alaska's seas and sank. As recently as 1980, the cruise ship *Prinsendam* caught fire in the Gulf of Alaska and sank. Alaska's waters are not to be taken lightly. ⚓ Even so, people continue to live, work, and play in Alaska's waters. The respect Alaskans have for the dangers and mysteries of its rivers, lakes, and seas is profound. The relationships Alaskans have with their boats, deep and abiding.

◄ ◄ An emergency response vessel shadows an oil tanker leaving Valdez.

◄ Sternwheeler *Discovery* III is reflected in the Chena River.

▲ Rafting makes a big splash on the Nenana River.

GETTING RID OF MOM

▲ The hulk of the *Princess Irene* sits in the small boat harbor of Tenakee Springs.
▶ A backyard boat parked in Ninilchik.

In New Guinea old boats are given regular burials, and the tools used to make them are put in the grave as funerary gifts. While I've never heard of anyone doing that here, Alaskans, nevertheless, develop some strange attachments to their boats. ⚓ Hulks of old boats dot the nearly 34,000 miles of rugged Alaska coastline. Some are shipwrecks left stuck on a rock or a beach where they may be too expensive and dangerous to retrieve. Many others are intentionally beached in coves or inlets, tied up in small boat harbors, or placed on blocks in the backyard awaiting repairs that will probably never come. Getting rid of an old car is one thing. Getting rid of something that bears the name of your mother,

wife, mistress, or girlfriend—regardless of her condition— is something else again. ⚓ There's a piece of maritime folk tradition that says no true sailor will ever demolish his wrecked vessel unless compelled to do so. In Alaska, where a person can become inexplicably attached to a piece of old duct tape, that tradition may be observed in its fullest flower.

◀ ◀ A trawler sits on the beach at St. Paul Island.
◀ A boat for sale in Homer.
◀ ▼ An old boat on the Homer Spit becomes a prophetic part of the landscape.
▼ A little "weekend" project waiting in Valdez.

A WHALE OF A TIME

▲ ▲ A bowhead whale graces
the sign of a Point Hope Inn.
▲ and ▶ A new sealskin
covering on an umiak requires
several weeks to dry.

For more than 2,000 years, the Iñupiat Eskimo have hunted the bowhead whale in seemingly fragile yet remarkably resilient boats called umiaks that are framed in wood and covered with the skins of bearded seal. The whaling season in Point Hope, located on the edge of the Chukchi Sea some 125 miles above the Arctic Circle, lasts only two months in the spring when the whales migrate north along the coast. Much preparation, however, takes place during the rest of the year. ⚓ Old boat coverings are replaced with new ones. Four or five bearded seal skins are sewn together with caribou sinew and fitted to the frame with sinew

or nylon rope and allowed to dry. Camouflage parkas made from polar bear fur are mended. Freight sleds, once pulled by dogs and now pulled by snowmobiles, are repaired and used to haul boats and equipment out onto the ice next to open water. Canvas tents, stoves, fuel, and food are readied for men who will live on the ice for weeks at a time. Rifles for protection against polar bears are checked and cleaned, and harpoons and rope go through annual maintenance. ⚓ As the time for the hunt approaches, anticipation grows. Hunting bowhead whales binds the people of Point Hope to each other and to their ancestors. It's the Super Bowl, the World Series, and the Fourth of July all rolled into one. ⚓ When the day comes and fog rises off newly-formed leads (openings) in the ice, the energy level in Point Hope pegs the meter. As one person in the village put it: "Work, play, family, health—everything comes to a stop for whale time."

◄ ▲ ATVs and snowmachines are the preferred mode of travel between the village and the whaling camps.

▲ Nalukataq (near Point Hope) is the site of annual whaling festivals in June.

DUCKY ON THE CHENA RIVER

Beginning in the mid-nineteenth century, hundreds of sternwheelers transported millions of tons of freight and thousands of adventure-hungry passengers from one gold rush city to another in interior Alaska. Sternwheelers were ideal for the shallow rivers of Alaska, possessing the ability to challenge wildly-fluctuating water levels, rocks, sandbars, snags, and shipboard fires. Their flat-bottomed design allowed them to literally bob on the water like a rubber ducky; a fully loaded sternwheeler traveled in water little deeper than needed by a heavily-laden canoe. ⚓ By the 1930s, as gold fever waned, sternwheeler towns like Fairbanks, Dawson City, Whitehorse, Circle, Forty-Mile, Eagle, and Ruby

▲ The *Discovery* III's sternwheel churns up the river twice daily.
▶ Early morning at Steamboat landing on the Chena River.

were little more than ghost towns. By the 1950s, the era of the sternwheeler was gone. ⚓ Jim Binkley, however, refused to let it go. The gold rush may have ended, but the tourism rush was just beginning. The son of a famous Alaska riverboat man, Jim built his first sternwheeler, the forty-nine-passenger *Discovery*, in his Fairbanks backyard in 1955. By 1959 he had lengthened her twice, once by cutting the boat in two, pulling it apart with a tractor, and fitting a new hull and superstructure in between. ⚓ Today the *Discovery III* carries up to 1,000 visitors at a time on tours along the Chena and Tanana rivers. Folks marvel at this reminder of Alaska's past, even if it does bob on the water like a rubber ducky.

◀ ◀ The sternwheeler *Discovery* III bobs along the Chena River.

B. O. A. T.

"They are expensive to keep," Fred Paulsen acknowledged as we stood in his boat yard in Petersburg watching the 75-foot *Northern Queen* rise slowly out of the water on the marine railway. "But you do get back out what you put in," he quickly added. "You have to keep on top of them." ⚓ Fred has been keeping on top of Southeast Alaska's pleasure and fishing boats at Petersburg Shipwrights, Inc. since 1980. "We don't have many empty days [on the railway], except in the darkest days of winter. We put in over 300 boats a

▲ The *Northern Queen* gets a ride on the marine railway.
▶ After a good wash and before repainting, the boat bottom gets a thorough drying.
▶ ▶ As part of an annual check-up, barnacles are removed from a boat's propeller.

year. ⚓ "Normally at this time of year [spring], all we do is annual maintenance: scrape and paint the bottom below waterline, that sort of thing. We've been doing the *Northern Queen* for about fifteen years," Fred added, pointing to the boat now high and dry in the yard. "It's sort of like a shave and a haircut." ⚓ And the cost of a shave and a haircut these days: about $2000 for a boat the size of the *Northern Queen*. "I just read in a magazine what the word boat really stands for," Fred told me with a grin. "Bring Out Another Thousand."

▲ Petersburg Shipwrights has been keeping boats in top form since 1980.
◀ Crab pots and floats make a colorful display in Petersburg.

HERRING ROE ROULETTE

▲ The roe is the thing in the sac roe herring fishery.
▶ Over fifty boats compete for an annual quota of 8,000 tons of herring roe.

In the sac roe herring fishery, it isn't the fish but the fish roe that is desired for the exclusively Japanese market. Unfortunately for the herring, fishermen harvest them just before they are ready to spawn in order to collect the roe. ⚓ For the fifty-one fishermen holding permits for the sac roe herring fishery in Sitka, an awful lot of money rides on a single throw of a purse seine net. With a boat capable of harvesting as much as 450 tons of herring in one set, an annual quota of 8,000 tons for the entire fishery can be reached in fairly short order. In fact, during an opening that can last as little as twenty minutes—a precaution necessary to prevent the boats from exceeding the total quota—one boat may earn as much as $500,000 while another boat, a few yards away, may come up empty.

Choosing the right spot to fish requires a skillful combination of science and luck. Jockeying for position with other boats trying to reach the same spot requires other skills. As one fisherman put it in a classic bit of understatement: "You gotta worry about the winds, another net, another boat, rocks . . . it's real hard."

▲ Herring roe is collected, processed, packed, and shipped almost exclusively for Japan.
◄ Purse seiners spend hours preparing for a fishery that may last as little as twenty minutes.

17

FUSSY WORK

"I love to build boats," John Lucking said to me. "I've thought of doing other things, but I always come back to boats." And what boats. John spends more than a hundred hours on each laminated canoe. While a lot of time is spent bending, fitting, and gluing the various pieces of spruce, cedar, mahogany, and ash together to form the shell, the bulk of the hours are spent completing the sanding and finishing to John's exacting standards. ⚓ "This is fussy work now," John told me as he sanded and re-sanded the boat several times as we talked. "I could put the thing in the water right now, but I wouldn't want to," he said shaking his head to indicate his disapproval with the boat's condition. ⚓ "I originally started this canoe to donate it to an organization for a fundraising auction, but I was embarrassed to do it," John confided, pointing to a five-square-inch area on the floor of the canoe that would be under the front seat. A few deep scratch marks showed in the sanded wood. ⚓ "I couldn't let this go as an example of my work."

▲ John Lucking fusses over the finish of one of his handmade canoes.
▶ More than 100 hours of work goes into the making of a laminated canoe.
▶ ▶ A John Lucking canoe made from spruce, cedar, mahogany, and ash is a thing of beauty.

DAVE'S DRIFTBOAT

▲ Dave has a dream of floating the Yukon River in a handmade boat.
▶ Dave struggles to translate his talent as a sculptor to boat building.
▶ ▶ "No one but no one would ever pay me to build a boat."

For Dave Present, floating the Yukon River from Whitehorse to Dawson has been a life-long dream. "My mother hated children's stories," Dave told me in the front yard of his Skagway home. "Growing up in Massachusetts, she read me Robert Service's poems about the Yukon and the Klondike Gold Rush. My dream was always to build my own boat just like the miners did and float down the river." ⚓ The 16-foot Glen-L driftboat— or dory as it may be called in some parts of the country—seemed the right choice because of its wide beam and ample freeboard. "I looked at the dimensions and thought this is perfect: untippable." ⚓ But dreaming about a boat and building one are two different things. "People think that because I'm an artist, a sculptor, the skills translate to boat building. They don't. I'm a lousy boat builder." ⚓ As we talked, Dave worked on the boat, alternately answering my questions and swearing to himself. "I don't think this will be an occupation," he said. "No one, but no one, would ever pay me to build a boat. But once I sand it, and paint it, and cover up some of my mistakes, it won't look too bad. And with a little luck, I may even make it to Dawson."

RUDOLPH'S REPLACEMENT

▲ Santa catches a ride aboard the M/V *LeConte*.
▶ A dad introduces his daughter to Santa.

Across the nation Santa rides a sleigh pulled by a bunch of reindeer, but not so in Southeast Alaska. Since the mid-eighties Santa travels by ferry, just like everybody else, requiring the better part of two weeks to visit places like Metlakatla, Wrangell, Petersburg, Haines, Tenakee Springs, and Skagway. ⚓ "For most kids this is the only chance they have to see Santa," said Tom Haas, one of several traveling Santas, on a trip aboard the M/V *LeConte* en route to Pelican, Angoon, and Hoonah. "Most times the kids come on board," Tom continued, "but sometimes we go to them." One time, when Santa

arrived in Angoon during school hours, Tom jumped on the ferry's luggage cart to drive up to the school and give away the magnets, candy canes, and key chains he carried in his red sack. ⚓ Tom has been a traveling Santa for years. "I started out with a borrowed Santa's suit," he said, "but now I've got one of my own." You could say it's a job Tom has grown into. "After all these years it doesn't take me very long to get into the suit—no padding or pillows needed. As a matter of fact, the way things are going, my wife may need to let it out a little."

◀ Santa enjoys a few hours of relaxation between stops in Southeast Alaska.

TRAIN WRECK, COFFEE GRINDER, & SPATTER ROCK

▲ Sybil and Rod Platt, dressed and ready to go on their raft trip.
▶ "Some people just want a boat ride, and some people are really into getting splashed."

Eleven-year-old Sybil Platt was offered a choice: a long bus ride in Denali National Park or a short raft trip on the Nenana River. For Sybil it was a no-brainer. ⚓ But there are raft trips and then there are RAFT TRIPS. The kind of trip Sybil and dad Rod would get on the Nenana, from the folks at the Denali Outdoor Center, was strictly up to the two of them. ⚓ "Some people just want a boat ride," long-time guide Carl Malatin told me, "and some people are really into getting splashed. We try to feel them out, find out what

they want, and give it to them." With names like Razorback, Train Wreck, Coffee Grinder, and Spatter Rock, plenty of rapids offer opportunities to get splashed during the two-hour trip. "We take people out and give them a sound thrashing," Carl continued. "If they want to get hammered, we hammer them." ⚓ After a short van ride to the head of Nenana Canyon, and a safety talk by guide John Hill, Sybil and her dad were ready to go. "Well, what do you think," John asked Sybil one last time, "wet ride or dry ride?" ⚓ "Wet!" Sybil exclaimed without hesitation. The look on dad's face showed less certainty.

◀ Rod Platt is thrown off balance by rapids.
▲ Another raft passes under the Nenana River Bridge.

TRUCKIN' IN THE SOUND

▲ Larry Gilman captains the M/V Itswoot.
▶ World-War-II-era landing craft were designed to go just about anywhere.

Twice a month aboard the World-War-II-era landing craft the M/V *Itswoot*, Larry Gilman and Chuck McDonald deliver groceries, mail, and equipment to a handful of fish hatcheries in Prince William Sound. ⚓ "You should see how much stuff we can get on this thing," said Larry as we stood in the pilothouse watching Chuck load pallets on board with a forklift. "Sometimes we'll be so low that water laps up under the gate. It actually rides better that way." ⚓ Though one would hardly call the *Itswoot* spacious, storage space was significantly increased after present owner Jerry Protzman widened the boat by four feet and lengthened it by twelve in 1978. With time these improvements have

become a bit obscured: "It doesn't look like they split it or lengthened it now that it's rusted evenly all over," Chuck observed. ⚓ Prince William Sound, in fact much of Alaska, is perfect for a craft designed to go where there are no docks, no wharfs, no anything. "It's a pretty neat piece of equipment," Chuck told me. "I drove trucks around Alaska at one time, now I drive this. Sometimes when it's shitty out here I get to wondering." He paused. "But overall I like the solitude."

▲ ◄ Though you would hardly call the *Itswoot* spacious, it hauls an amazing amount of stuff.
▲ The *Itswoot* delivers supplies to fish hatcheries in Prince William Sound.
◄ Chuck McDonald enjoys the solitude aboard the *Itswoot*.

EUPHORIUM II

Ever since the float houses moved into Mud Bay north of Ketchikan in the mid-seventies, they have been the source of controversy. ⚓ "About eight different state and federal agencies are interested in them," Wayne Ward, a past owner of one of the float houses known as Euphorium II, told me. "Every two or three years someone new comes along

▲ The Spenser family calls the Euphorium II home.
▶ The float houses of Mud Bay have been a source of controversy since the mid-seventies.

◄ There used to be two houses on the float, but a couple of guys living in one burned the other for firewood.

and decides the 'outlaw' float houses have to go. After a while, the official goes away." ⚓ The Euphorium II has had at least seven owners including the present owners, Lisa and Jerad Spenser, and Lois and Wayne Ward— Lisa's mom and dad. Just about everyone who has lived there has left his or her mark on the place. According to Lisa, the biggest changes were made one winter by a couple of tenants. "There were originally two houses on the float," Lisa told me, "but the guys living in one of the houses burned the other one for firewood." ⚓ A construction project on nearby North Tongass Highway threatens the Mud Bay float houses once again. "They're planning to put the new embankment through the living room," said Jerad. ⚓ The "powers-that-be" may want the Euphorium II out of Mud Bay, but Wayne has other plans. "I'll move the house out into the bay, wait until they finish, and then move it right back in place. I love that house. I love that life style."

PILLAGE IN PETERSBURG

▲ Every year Vikings invade Petersburg as part of the local Little Norway Festival.
▶ The Viking ship *Valhalla* sails the streets of Petersburg.

One weekend a year, during The Little Norway Festival, Vikings invade Petersburg, a small fishing community of 3,500 on Mitkof Island in Southeast Alaska founded by Norwegian Peter Buschmann. Since 1978 the Viking ship *Valhalla* with a bloodthirsty (or just plain thirsty) crew of Vikings and Valkyries has sailed the waterways and streets of Petersburg as the centerpiece of this celebration of Norway's Constitution Day. ⚓ The 30-foot-long *Valhalla*, however, wasn't built for the festival or even in Petersburg for that

matter, but in Keyport, New Jersey to sail in the Festival of Tall Ships held in New York Harbor as part of our nation's Bicentennial. ⚓ When word reached Petersburg that the *Valhalla* needed a new home, the festival committee snatched it up. The boat got passed around a bit before finally finding a home with the Sons of Norway, a Norwegian Fraternal Organization. ⚓ For the first few years, Vikings with names like Tarvol the Twisted and Vulgär the Crude sailed the *Valhalla* two to three miles down the nearby Wrangell Narrows during the festival. "She sailed real nice," Dale Rose, a Sons of Norway member said, "but I always had to drag her back to town behind my boat because the Vikings got too drunk." ⚓ About three years ago the cost of insurance for one day of Viking pillage got too high, and the boat has sailed down the main street of town in the festival parade ever since. "Little Vikings and Valkyries ride inside the boat now," Dale said. "The big Vikings walk alongside for crowd control."

◀ Everybody becomes Norwegian at least once a year.
▶ Petersburg has a distinctly Norwegian personality.

29

HAVE A FERRY NICE FLIGHT

▲ At the best of times, a trip to the airport can be a trying experience.
▶ Eighteen hours a day, 365 days a year, a ferry transports passengers to and from the Ketchikan airport.

Even at the best of times, a trip to the airport can tire and frustrate you. For the folks in Ketchikan, add another entirely unique possibility: you may get seasick. ⚓ Ketchikan International Airport is on Gravina Island, separated some 600 yards from the rest of Ketchikan on Revillagigedo Island. When construction began on the airport in the early seventies, plans included a bridge. But as the project progressed and ran low on funds, the bridge was shelved "temporarily" in favor of a lower-cost ferry option. ⚓ Eighteen hours a day, 365 days a year, the sixteen-vehicle M/V *Bob Ellis* and its smaller sister ferry the nine-vehicle M/V *Ken Eichnrer* (or is that brother ferry), transport passengers and vehicles back and forth across the Tongass Narrows. Has the weather ever stopped a ferry from making the trip? "Not a chance," said ferry deckhand Shawn Able. "Last winter we had 100 MPH winds and we still went out."

DONALD'S DOUBLE-ENDER

When it comes to rescuing old things from the junk pile of history, Donald Brusehaber is an ace. Over the years he has restored old marine engines, salvaged farm implements, rescued old lamps and fish floats, recycled building materials and telephone poles, and even found uses for some old broken bottles. Today he is preparing to save a barn dating to 1830 in his hometown of Orchard Park, New York, take it apart, and reassemble it on his five acres in Eagle River. Likewise, a few years ago, when Donald had a chance to save an old Bristol Bay fishing boat from a one-way trip to the land fill, he jumped at the opportunity. "A friend bought the boat and set it out on his front lawn," said Donald. "His wife wasn't too pleased. Eventually he told me, 'If you want the boat, take it; otherwise, it's going to the dump.' I took it." ⚓ Donald figures the boat dates to the 1920s when 28-foot, double-ender sailboats commonly plied the waters of Bristol Bay in search

of salmon. "It still has bits of paint on it that were the colors of the Alaska Packers Association. It's a piece of history. You can't just throw it away." ⚓ He admits that turning the boat into a garden gazebo was more a short-term act of salvation than a display of creative inspiration. "Getting it off the ground was the most important thing," he continued. "If you keep it dry, it will last a long time." ⚓ And where will the boat from Bristol Bay wind up? "Once I get that barn rebuilt," Donald said, "I'll hang the boat in it."

▲ This old lantern is one of many things Donald Brusehaber has saved from the junk pile of history.
◀ A 1920s era double-end sailboat performs temporary duty as a garden gazebo.

COHO COWBOY

"Alaska was always my dream," Al Rule told me while we rode his 36-foot gill-netter the F/V *Seahorse* out into the Copper River Delta in search of coho (silver) salmon. Originally from Colorado, Al came to Cordova in 1976. He took the $400 he saved from working all summer in a cannery and bought his first boat, a skiff. His buddy loaned him an outboard, and he was set; he's been fishing ever since. ⚓ Gillnets entangle salmon: it's a more effective technique for the shallow murky waters of the delta than the more common purse seine which corrals them. "When the tide goes out, the salmon get confused and start swimming in circles," Al explained. "You set up in a spot which is going to narrow down as the tide drops and you wait." ⚓ Attached to one end of the net is a float with a battery-powered light. The float is dropped overboard, and the boat is backed up to pay

▲ and ▶ Al Rule cruises the Copper River Delta in his gill-netter searching for coho salmon.

▲ Gillnets entangle salmon instead of coralling them.
◀ Gill netting for coho salmon is a tedious process that's repeated over and over for hours on end.

out the net. Floats hold one edge of the net at the surface while weights keep the other edge down. After a span of time, which may vary from a few minutes to hours, the net is reeled back on board and the fish are removed by hand, one at a time. It is a time-consuming and tedious process that's repeated over and over again: six fish the first set, twenty fish the second, three fish the third, twelve fish the fourth, and on and on and on. . . . ⚓ Near the close of the allotted twenty-four-hour fishing period—called an "opening"—Al decided to call it a day. His catch weighed in at 707 pounds, just $353.50. "If they had been sockeyes," Al said, "they would have been worth $1,500, but not silvers. You got to put a lot of silvers together at fifty cents a pound to make something."

KAASDA HEENI— CANOE FROM INDIAN RIVER

▲ Cedar is used for totem poles as well as dugout canoes.
▶ Operating a canoe at peak efficiency requires practice.

Anthropologists believe that the earliest boats may have been floating logs which were eventually made more seaworthy by scooping out the interior to form a shell. These dugout canoes have been common in cultures around the world for thousands of years, but nowhere has the dugout been developed to such a degree of sophistication as the Tlingit canoe of Southeast Alaska. ⚓ Unfortunately, over the course of the twentieth century, the sophisticated skills needed to make a ceremonial Tlingit canoe were nearly lost. In 1988, to help revive those skills—and Tlingit culture in Sitka as well—the Southeast Alaska Indian Cultural Center, with the assistance of a grant from the National

Endowment for the Arts, commissioned the first red cedar canoe to be built in Sitka since 1904. ⚓ Working at the Sitka National Historical Park headquarters, carvers Wayne Price, Will Burkhardt, and Tommy Joseph took eight months to carve the graceful 37-foot canoe. The canoe was steamed into final shape on a beach near the mouth of the Indian River, using an ancient technique in which the canoe is filled with water heated to boiling by hot rocks. Paint was applied later at park headquarters. ⚓ On May 8, 1999, people from around Alaska came to Sitka to participate in the dedication and naming of the new canoe. In a ceremony that was part political rally, part block party, and part christening, this "new addition" was introduced to the community: Kaasda Heeni—The Canoe from Indian River.

◀ ▲ The 37-foot canoe was carved from a single cedar log.

◀ ◀ Tlingit culture is alive and well in Sitka.

◀ In a ceremony that was part political rally, part block party, and part christening, the new canoe was introduced to the community.

GOLD BOAT

▲ Even today, it's hard to resist gold fever.
▶ A gold dredge could tear through as much gravel in a day as a thousand prospectors.

When most people think of gold mining in Alaska, they picture a lone prospector bent over a creek with gold pan in hand. However, during Alaska's most productive mining period in the early 1900s, it was the gold dredge, not the prospector, that was the most common sight in mining country. Sometimes called "Gold Boats," and "metal mastodons," the gold dredge could tear through as much gravel in a day as a thousand prospectors working with pick and shovel. For good or ill, the gold dredge did for gold mining what Henry Ford did for building cars. ⚓ In Mary Lee Davis's 1930 book *Uncle Sam's Attic*, she describes a gold dredge as: ". . . a large scow with heavy machinery and housing on it, floating in a little pond of water which it opens ahead by digging in and closes up behind as it edges slowly along the creek bottom—like some prehistoric monster reaching out its long neck of chain and buckets, rooting in the earth with its metal snout, and drawing in enormous meals of golden gravels." ⚓ I couldn't have said it better myself.

SPINS, SUCKHOLES, & STUBBY KAYAKS

▲ Every year kayaks gather at Sixmile Creek for three days of races.

▶ The trick is to perform spins, rolls, and cartwheels and to look good while doing them.

After the first white-water rodeo on Idaho's Salmon River in 1976, "rodeo" took on a whole new meaning. No longer just a matter of riding, roping, and bucking broncs, now we have suckholes, pop-ups, and enders. ⚓ Alaska has white-water rodeos too. Every year a hardy group of kayakers gather at Sixmile Creek on the Kenai Peninsula for the annual Gene Shumar Memorial PaddleFest: three days of races, boat tricks, and beer. ⚓ Unlike a rodeo of the cowboy kind, a kayaker's rodeo involves performing a number of spins, rolls, and cartwheels in a cauldron of white water. The manuevers are intended to show off a competitor's courage as much as his hot-dogging abilities. Surviving in thrashing 36° water is one thing; looking good for the judges while you are doing it is something else again. ⚓ The boats used for these "play" events are not your sleek touring kayaks built for comfort and stability. These short and stubby kayaks— 12 foot or less—are designed for maneuver-ability and responsiveness. When you're floating upside down through mammoth waves, and these guys seem to do that a lot, righting yourself as quickly as possible has some importance. How well a kayaker fits his kayak determines how quickly a rollover can be corrected; you don't sit in one of these kayaks as much as wear one.

BLESSING THE BOATS

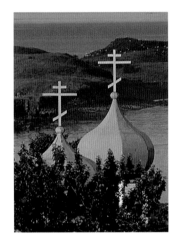

▲ The Russian Orthodox Church established a parish in Kodiak in 1794.
▶ and ▶▶ Blessing the boats has been an annual event for many years.

Fishing is a dangerous occupation, and the North Pacific waters around Kodiak Island are one of the most dangerous places in the world to fish. Hundreds of Kodiak's boats work the open ocean around the Gulf of Alaska and the Bering Sea to harvest salmon, halibut, cod, pollock, dungeness crab, opillio crab, and king crab. Last year alone, seventeen residents out of a population of 14,000 died at sea. So it should be no surprise that when it comes to asking for a little help, these folks never look a gift blessing in the mouth. ⚓ The Russian Orthodox Church, which established a parish in Kodiak in 1794, offers an annual blessing of boats and crews. "Blessing boats here goes way back," said Fr. Dunlop, standing near the Church of the Holy Resurrection. "We probably started the blessing from the inception of the parish." ⚓ Each year dozens of boats, from trawlers to kayaks, pass close to the ferry dock along Near Island Channel to receive a splash or two of holy water and a prayer for the safety of the boat, crew, and gear. For fishermen, a wish for a full hold of fish is thrown in for good measure. As one captain said while he prepared to line up with the other boats: "It can't hurt."

SANTA SACRILEGE IN SEWARD

▲ A one-eyed Santa holds a beer aboard the *Florette* C.
▶ Dianne had to choose between the boat and a boyfriend. She kept the boat.

Dianne Dubuc has loved just about every minute aboard the F/V *Florette C* since she bought the salmon charter boat in 1989. "I had the boat and I had a boyfriend for nine years," she said. "He wanted me to sell the boat and buy a laundromat." There was a pause. "I still have the boat." ⚓ A lot of work has gone into the 53-foot Fiberglas boat since Dianne decided to live on board in 1995, and it's the kind of work appreciated by those who know boats. "I was in Cordova a while ago," Dianne told me, "and they know

boats. I was there for ten days and got three marriage proposals." Little wonder with a boat that includes a washer/dryer, a forced-air furnace, a kitchen with range and oven, and a bathroom complete with small bathtub. For Dianne, life aboard her floating home is much like life just about anywhere, if you discount the fact that her home can sink. ⚓ The final step in making her boat a home came with the addition of Christmas lights. "A friend in town volunteered to be my decorating committee," she said. Foley (her committee), Mike (her crew), and Dianne decorated the boat in about three hours. "Foley went to the top of the mast in winds that topped 40 MPH."

⚓ Despite her efforts, the *Florette C* wasn't even recognized in a competition for the best Christmas lights in town. "I don't think they liked Santa holding a beer can and a patch over his eye," Dianne said. "I guess they thought I had committed Santa sacrilege."

◄ The *Florette* C is more than just a charter fishing boat—it's Dianne Dubuc's home.

KAYAKS BY THE DOZEN

▲ Unloading gear from one of two chartered boats at Culross Island.
▶ A group of women make a "guy-less" kayak trip in Prince William Sound every year.

"We wanted to do something challenging, some wilderness thing without the guys," Cathy Hart told me, describing the first kayak trip she and six of her female friends made in Prince William Sound back in 1992. "We hired someone to give us a session in a pool so that we would be safe," she continued, "and we invited someone along who knew what she was doing to act as a guide." ⚓ No one gave much thought beyond that first trip; afterward, everyone was hooked. They have been making at least one trip a year ever since, and many of the women now own their own kayaks. Over time, some women have been added and a few subtracted. While not everyone has initially known each other, they all know Cathy. ⚓ "I think about the stuff we did that first two-day trip," Cathy said with a big grin on her face. "We took enough food to last all summer. Laurie, the guide, was going to teach us how to hang our food to keep it away from

bears, but we couldn't find a tree big enough to support it." ⚓ Cathy and I spoke while riding in one of two chartered boats headed across Prince William Sound to Culross Island. Accompanying Cathy on this year's trip were three Debbies, one Kathy, two Karens, one Polly, one Jeannie, one Susan, one Brenda, one Bunny, their twelve kayaks, and a whole lot of gear. I was invited along for the ride to the island as long as I promised not to stay.

◄ Taking a break at the beach camp on Culross Island.
▲ An example of the local wildlife.

FLOATING CITIES

▲ A cruise ship dominates the Skagway skyline.
▶ Ships have brought visitors to Skagway since the days of the Klondike Gold Rush.

If 8,000 visitors suddenly appeared in my Brooklyn neighborhood while I was growing up, I'm not sure I would have noticed. But in a place like Skagway, population 800, located at the northern end of Southeast Alaska's Inside Passage, it's harder for that number of visitors to simply blend in. ⚓ Ships have brought visitors to Skagway since the days of the Klondike Gold Rush in 1898. Back then, a steamer might deliver a couple of hundred gold seekers bound for the gold fields near Dawson City, Yukon. Over the eighteen-month peak of the gold rush, historians estimate that as many as 100,000 people from around the world headed to the Klondike. Most came through Skagway, which at its busiest boasted a population approaching 10,000. Lots of those folks never got closer to

the gold fields than the north end of town. They arrived in Skagway, soaked up a little of the gold rush ambiance, and returned home. ⚓ The gold rush may be over, but visitors continue to seek a little gold rush ambiance. On a busy day, six of these floating cities can deliver 8,000 people to Skagway's waterfront before noon. Although they are back on board and out of town by 9:00 P.M., Skagway is transformed, at least temporarily, from a small town into Alaska's sixth largest city.

◄, ▲▲ and ▲ Thousands of people a day visit Skagway to soak up a little gold rush ambiance.

TWO-HUNDRED-TON PTARMIGAN

▲ Tom Callahan, captain of the *Ptarmigan*.
▶ The M/V *Ptarmigan* "rules" Portage Lake.
▶ ▶ Passengers aboard the *Ptarmigan* get an up-close view of Portage Glacier.

After completing about 500 four-mile round trips on Portage Lake, you have to forgive Captain Tom Callahan's attempts at humor. "We rule the lake," he declared during what might have been his 501st trip to the face of Portage Glacier, one of Alaska's star attractions located just fifty miles south of Anchorage. "Of course we are the only boat allowed on the lake." ⚓ All boats, even canoes and kayaks, were banned from the commonly iceberg-choked waters of the lake for many years. In the late-eighties, Holland America Cruises was granted the sole right to offer an up-close look at the glacier. To do the job as

safely and as unobtrusively as possible, they built a rather peculiarly-shaped, white-painted vessel. ⚓ "This is the only boat I've been on where people ask which end is the front," Captain Tom said. "I've been tempted to back it up all the way to the glacier to see if anyone notices." ⚓ In the mid-nineties, with little to no warning, the Portage Glacier retreated to a spot where it rarely calves anymore—leaving the lake virtually ice free—and leaving a certain white, 80-foot long, 220-ton, 200-passenger ship named for an Alaska bird known for its camouflage ability about as unobtrusive as . . . well, a 200-ton ptarmigan.

MARION'S PRIDE & JOY

After twelve years of restoration work, Marion Beck takes a lot of pride in the *Danny J.* It's well deserved. The transition from open WWII ship-to-shore troop transport to Kachemak Bay ferry has been a long one. Along the way the boat hauled lumber and freight, served as a tender for a purse seiner, and had a stint as a gill-netter. Sometime, no one knows exactly when anymore, the *Danny J* was closed in and a pilothouse built on. ⚓ Marion started running the ferry in 1974 and bought it in 1980. "At first we did runs to Jackaloff Bay, Halibut Cove, and all places in between," she said. "We hauled a lot of

▲ The *Danny* J carries locals and visitors between Homer and Halibut Cove every summer.
▶ Twelve years of restoration work was required to transform the old *Danny* J into the boat it is today.

freight then. When we got to Halibut Cove, everyone got off and had tea at my parent's house." ⚓ Eventually service was limited to Halibut Cove and Homer. Now the *Danny J* carries a few boat-less Halibut Cove residents, a bit of supplies, and lots of curious visitors from Memorial Day to Labor Day—always under Marion's watchful eye. ⚓ "I used to tow logs with this boat," Marion said shaking her head, "but not since I redid her. Now I get upset if someone ties up alongside."

▲ Marion Beck gets a minute to visit with a passenger aboard the *Danny* J.
◄ Sometime, no one knows when, the pilot house was added to the old WWII-era boat.

CANOE CONUNDRUM

▲ Checking a map along the Yukon River in an effort to figure out where the heck I am.
▶ When it came time to make a choice between indestructibility and aesthetics, I chose an indestructible, aluminum canoe.

When the time came for me to choose between a Grumman aluminum or a classic, wooden, Old Town canoe for my 2,000 mile trip down the Yukon River in 1976, it was a bit like choosing between a tank and a racy sports car. For a guy from Brooklyn, New York about to make his first solo canoe trip through the Alaska and Canadian wilderness, choosing indestructibility over aesthetics seemed the way to go. ⚓ Of course traveling in a metal canoe in 36° water was a bit cold, and the constant rasping of the silted river

against the hull was noisy. But when it came to dragging that fully-loaded boat in and out of the river, over rocks and gravel, at least twice a day, for nearly three months, I was glad I didn't care two figs about the bottom. Then there was that time near the Arctic Circle when a young grizzly inspected the canoe's interior with his teeth. Anyway, I never had a bit of food spoil in the refrigerator-like bottom, and even the rasping sound eventually faded into the background. ⚓ I did worry what I was going to do with the canoe at the end of my trip. But I discovered when I reached the lower part of the river that folks coveted small indestructible boats like mine for duck hunting. A thousand miles from the nearest boat dealer, I had a hot commodity. In fact I'm sure if I had floated the river with a half-dozen of those things strung out behind me, I could have sold them all.

◀ An eighty-eight=day river trip required quite a bit of gear.
▲ Sunset on the Yukon.

SPANKY'S ONE-MINUTE RIDE

▲ Fishermen wait to make the one-minute ferry crossing of the Kenai River.
▶ Katie "Spanky" Walter helps passengers board the Kenai River ferry.

Each year thousands of fishermen with a glint in their eyes and a rod in their hands come to Copper Landing for a chance to stand elbow to elbow and fish for salmon at the confluence of the Kenai and Russian Rivers. The Sterling Highway may bring them close, but no road will actually deliver them to the promised land; only a one-minute ferry ride will do that. ⚓ The Kenai River ferry, which looks more like a D-Day landing craft, requires a crew of two: a skipper licensed by the Coast Guard at the wheel and a deckhand who ties off the ferry at either end and assists in loading and unloading passengers. At peak season, the ferry makes about seventy trips a day. ⚓ "I'm seeing this stretch of river a whole bunch," said deckhand Katie "Spanky" Walter. "Some days it's a little too

much. And then it's like, you've just taken a load across, you look back, and there's a person waiting. You just can't win," she shrugged. "They're all so impatient." ⚓ Though emotions sometimes run hot, the mechanics that make the 240-foot ride possible are really cool. "The ferry's flat bottomed with no rudder, no engine, nothing," explained skipper Rick Holben. "It's like sailing. You turn a large steel wheel on the stern that turns a screw on the back that pulls ropes anchored on either side of the ferry. You just angle the stern into the current, and away she goes."

▲ Fishermen stand elbow to elbow along the banks of the Kenai River.
◄ The Kenai River ferry, which resembles a D-Day landing craft, requires a crew of two.

THE GREATEST RACE YOU NEVER HEARD OF

▲ The crew works hard to keep this river boat from literally taking flight.
▶ Boats in the Yukon 800 Race travel at speeds exceeding 70 mph.

The Yukon 800 may be the oldest, the toughest, and the longest river boat race in the world, but you won't be able to watch it on ESPN or read about it in *Sports Illustrated*. The homegrown race, held around the summer solstice since 1960, is definitely one of Alaska's best-kept secrets. ⚓ Twenty-four-foot-long, three-person, ultra-streamlined, handmade, wooden boats are made from quarter-inch plywood, Sitka Spruce, and duct tape and fitted with 50 hp outboards. They race in two tortuous 400-mile heats along the Chena, Tanana, and Yukon rivers—from Fairbanks to Galena and back—at speeds exceeding 70 MPH. These boats are not to be confused with your basic riverboat. When the navigator isn't helping the skipper find the best route through twisting river channels, and the engineer isn't pushing the engine to operate at 110 percent, you can find the crew leaning far over one rail or the other, sometimes only inches above the surface, to keep the 175-pound boat from literally taking flight. ⚓ But speed alone doesn't win the Yukon 800. According to Wes Alexander, a five-time winner: "You have to compete with the river more than with the other racers. The river throws sticks. It switches channels. It throws you off to gravel bars and sweepers [trees leaning out from the bank very close to the water]. It can break your boat in two. Anything can happen; and you have to be ready to beat it all."

RED GREEN RIVER REGATTA

▲, ▼ and ▼ ► A good dose of creativity, and the use of at least one roll of duct tape, are requirements for the annual regatta.

"This could be real embarrassing," Bob Friend remarked as he looked at the competition parked along the bank of the Chena River in Fairbanks. The Volkswagen Beetle mounted on fuel drums looked formidable. The two-person double sink, stealthy. The bicycle-driven, Styrofoam paddlewheel, ingenious. ⚓ Bob and his four-person crew were about to enter the third annual Red Green River Regatta: a two-and-one-half mile "race" in which creativity in construction, the use of at least one roll of duct tape—Bob used three—and the ability to keep your boat afloat are more important than winning. ⚓ "I named the boat the SS *Bird*, so in case we flipped we would have something funny to say," Bob told me. "I just hope nothing happens to Armie," he continued, pointing to the stuffed armadillo strapped to the front of the boat. "I've had this guy for twenty years." ⚓ After a rocky start, the SS *Bird* completed the regatta in just over two hours, finishing a respectable fifth in a field of fourteen entries. "Everything was cool," Bob said with obvious pride at the Pike's Landing finish line. "We'll be doing it again next year with a few minor improvements." ⚓ I'm not sure whether Bob was referring to the SS *Bird* or its crew.

SHADOW SHIP

For Prevention and Response Specialist Jeffrey Keebler aboard the *Pioneer Service,* the old adage "no news is good news" is always true. ⚓ Like a fussy aunt trailing behind a two-year-old with mop in hand, the *Pioneer Service* closely follows oil tankers from the marine terminal in Valdez to the Hinchinbrook Entrance in the Gulf of Alaska, a distance of more than sixty miles. And when I say closely, I mean closely. In Valdez Narrows, the *Pioneer Service* stays within one-tenth of a mile. Elsewhere in the sound, the distance is

▲ Jeffrey Keebler's job is to watch for anything out of the ordinary.
▶ The ERV *Pioneer Service* shadows a loaded tanker as it approaches Valdez Narrows.

increased to one-quarter mile. ⚓ Since the *Exxon Valdez* ran aground on Bligh Reef in 1989 and put more than ten million gallons of crude oil into Prince William Sound, folks have been a little nervous about letting loaded tankers travel unescorted. Should the unthinkable ever be repeated, Jeffrey would take charge as the on-scene Task Force Leader and assign his ten crew members to contain as much of the spill as possible. ⚓ "I have never been on an escort where I thought I would use the equipment," Jeffrey told me. I hope he never will.

◀ Emergency response vessels were designed to contain as much oil as possible as quickly as possible.
▲ ▲ No news is good news for the crew of the *Pioneer Service*.
▲ Stellar sea lions on a navigation buoy near Valdez Narrows.

PETER'S PICKUP

"Most people couldn't live here without one," Peter Mooney said over the din of his engine. "It's not a matter of using them for sport. You want one that's pretty damn good; one you can have faith in when you're out in bad weather." In many places Peter might have been discussing the old family pickup. But in Port Alexander, a tiny fishing village on the south end of Baranof Island in Southeast Alaska, Peter was talking about something else: the old family skiff. ⚓ Surrounded by water and with no roads, the skiff—a boat that's less than twenty feet long, aluminum, with an outboard motor—may be all the transportation that's available. It's part pickup, part family sedan, part delivery truck. Folks do without a telephone, television, electricity, or running water, but a skiff is

▲ Transporting supplies is just one of many jobs for the family skiff.
▶ Winnie the dog barks at the waves as Peter drives his skiff on an errand.

indispensable. ⚓ Sadly, the Alaskan skiff, like the automobile, is often taken for granted, unless you are a teenager without one. For a teen, owning your first "ride" is a major adolescent milestone, be it a 1952 Chevy Bel Air Deluxe two-tone sedan (I still miss that car) or a beat-up Lund skiff with an old Mercury outboard. ⚓ "Just like beater pickups, there are beater skiffs," Peter said as we toured Port Alexander in his 16-foot Lund skiff along with Winnie the dog. "But once they start leaking, that's pretty much the end. Even teenagers get tired of bailing out their boats."

▲ With no roads and surrounded by water, skiffs are indispensable in Port Alexander.
◄ In this Southeast Alaska community, the school bus is really a school boat.

STAR OF KODIAK

When a catastrophic earthquake destroyed much of Kodiak in 1964, leaving one of the busiest fishing ports in the country without a shore-based processor, the Alaska Packers Association turned to the War Shipping Administration's mothball fleet in Olympia, Washington for a temporary fix. The *Albert M. Boe*, the last Liberty ship built in World War II, was refitted for fish processing, renamed *Star of Kodiak*, and towed to its new, stationary home on the waterfront. ⚓ When war broke out in Europe in 1939, an American merchant fleet was practically non-existent. A fleet of ships, built quickly and cheaply by mostly unskilled labor, was needed to haul millions of tons of men, food, and war materials. Between 1941 and 1945, the United States built 2,710 Liberty ships at shipyards around the country. While the first one required 245 days to complete, a special effort in

▲ The *Star of Kodiak* was the last Liberty ship built in World War II.
▶ After more than thirty-five landlocked years, the *Star of Kodiak* has become a permanent feature of the Kodiak waterfront.

September 1942 cut construction time to just fifteen days. ⚓ After the war many of the ships were converted to cargo service around the world. Others, like the *Albert M. Boe*, were mothballed. Although Liberty ships weren't built for long-time service, many survived into the 1960s until metal fatigue forced them onto the scrap heap. ⚓ Kodiak's temporary solution has survived construction booms, urban renewals, and at least one fire, to become a permanent fixture on the downtown waterfront. In fact, the *Star of Kodiak* may be the last of the Liberty ships in use today.

◄ and ▲ Kodiak is one of the busiest fishing ports in the United States.

POOR MAN'S CRUISE SHIP

▲ You can find people aboard the ferry sleeping at almost anytime and almost anywhere.
▶ Traveling by ferry is definitely not for the person who is in a rush.

Locals call them "The Blue Canoes," and most visitors who ride the seven vessels of the Alaska Marine Highway System in Southeast Alaska know them as the poor man's cruise ship. But you won't find long-legged dancers performing in the cabaret or French wines served in the dining room of these "cruise ships." In fact, on most of the ferries, the best you will do is a snack bar. ⚓ Traveling by ferry is definitely not for the person who is in a rush. In twenty-five years of ferry riding, I don't remember ever passing another vessel, unless you count one-man kayaks. At an average speed of fifteen knots and with stops along the way, the 375-mile trip from Ketchikan to Haines can take 30 hours—barring delays caused by tides, breakdowns, and the not-so-simple task of unloading and loading

cars, trucks, vans, RVs, trailers, boats, and motorcycles at every stop. ⚓ So what do you do for all those hours? Reading and eating are big. Sleeping is probably bigger. You can find people sleeping at almost any time and almost anywhere: in one of the tiny staterooms on all but two of the ferries, on the floor of the observation lounge, sitting at a table in the snack bar, or stretched out on deck. Young people with backpacks and veteran ferry travelers (like me) gravitate to the solarium to stake a claim on a reclining lounge chair, or if space permits, erect a free-standing tent for a little extra privacy. ⚓ But mostly people sit and watch Alaska roll by. With thousands of square miles of mountains, forests, and glaciers to look at, who can blame them? It's the perfect way to pass the time.

◀ ▲ Locals call the seven ferries in Southeast Alaska "The Blue Canoes."
▲ Most people on the ferry just sit and watch Alaska roll by.

LAST WORD

After completing my first two books, *Outhouses of Alaska* and *Log Cabins of Alaska*, people would say things like: "Gee I wish I had talked to you when you were working on the book. I know this great outhouse you would have loved," or, "How come you didn't include my Uncle Charlie's cabin in your book? Everybody knows it." I'm sure this book will bring the same reaction. ⚓ Deciding which stories to include was a struggle. I included as many types of boats as possible, and I tried to use each story to say something different about the relationships Alaskans have with them. Ultimately, I suppose it was a matter of time and money; you can only travel to so many places and take so much time. ⚓ Finding and photographing boats for this book presented a number of challenges I didn't have to face with outhouses and log cabins. To be sure, some of the boats included here were found using the same tried and true method I used previously: blind luck. But

▶ Harry M. Walker leaned heavily on past experience and blind luck to find the boats included in this book.

while outhouses and log cabins tend to stay in one spot year round, not so for boats. Seasons, weather, fish, and mammal migrations were all factors that needed to be considered. Inevitably I spent months crisscrossing the state to be in the right place at the right time. ⚓ I wouldn't have changed the experience for the world.

64